I0794485

Jill's First Game

by Aiden Johnson
illustrated by Audrey Durney

Practice Decodable 81

McGraw Hill Education

Bothell, WA • Chicago, IL • Columbus, OH • New York, NY

MHEonline.com

Copyright © 2015 McGraw-Hill Education

All rights reserved. No part of this publication may be reproduced or distributed in any form or by any means, or stored in a database or retrieval system, without the prior written consent of McGraw-Hill Education, including, but not limited to, network storage or transmission, or broadcast for distance learning.

Send all inquiries to:
McGraw-Hill Education
8787 Orion Place
Columbus, OH 43240-4027

ISBN: 978-0-02-139016-8
MHID: 0-02-139016-9

Printed in China.

8 9 10 11 12 DSS 27 26 25 24 23

Dad had to go on a trip. He would miss Jill's first baseball game. He sadly reminded Jill.

Jill knew that Dad felt sad. "I will tell you a replay of the game," she said.

"Super!" said Dad. "Do not tell me the replay on the phone. Tell me when I get home."

On his trip, Dad thought and rethought about his first baseball game. His dad and mom saw him play.

Dad was returning home. Inside the plane, Dad still felt sad. He had missed Jill's first game!

"Jill is in the backyard. She cannot wait to replay the game for you," Mom said.

Jill had on her team shirt. She had a tee and a bat. She was ready for the replay!

Jill placed a ball on the tee. Then she replaced it. It had to be just right.

"Dad, it was cloudy. Before the game, Coach Jean retold us the rules," said Jill.

Coach Jean always repeated the rules. She did not like improper play.

"When the game started, I was first at bat," said Jill.

Jill was rethinking about what happened next.

"I swung and missed," said Jill. "I reset my feet for the next swing."

"Then rain fell! It was impossible to play! We ran inside!" said Jill.

Dad looked surprised.

"We will replay the game this morning!" said Jill. Dad would get to see Jill's first game!